Kingdom
of Curious Creatures

A FAIRYTALE
ADVENTURE
BOOK

Kanoko Egusa

T0046746

A group of curious babies

were born in the bountiful countryside.

Ducklings who chased after their mother on days out,

kittens who played on the grass together,

and cheerful rabbits and frogs

who enjoyed swimming in the sea.

Surrounded by their friends and given plenty of love,

the babies grew quickly and soon became adults,

then moved to their dream city: Paris.

Dressing up in their favorite clothes and shopping at boutiques,

visiting cafés and having tea with their friends,

and sometimes courageously setting out to foreign lands . . .

Every day was filled with joy and adventure,

excitement and wonder!

Prepare to explore the beautiful

Kingdom of Curious Creatures.

About the Author

Kanoko Egusa |ILLUSTRATOR, ARTIST

Kanoko Egusa was born in Sendai, Japan. After graduating from university, she studied professional design and drawing at a vocational school in Kanazawa and started to work as a freelance graphic designer in 2008. In 2011, she began kanoko egusa design atelier, creating illustrations depicting imaginary worlds filled with animals, flowers, and plants.

In her studio, Kanoko surrounds herself with the things and images that inspire her. She takes inspiration from nature and from antique books, postcards, and greeting cards. One of her favorite artists is John Tenniel, and she's studied the style and technique of his illustrations for *Alice's Adventures in Wonderland*. As a child she enjoyed the *Tom and Jerry* show, Disney films, Beatrix Potter's *The Tale of Peter Rabbit*, and Tasha Tudor's illustrated children's books.

Kanoko begins each piece of art simply, hand drawing using a dip pen and ink. She then digitizes each illustration to make any adjustments and finishing touches. With each illustration, she seeks to capture vivid expressions and magical moments, full of emotion and life.

Look for Kanoko's other fully illustrated coloring book

Garden of Fairytale Animals

Journey to a magical garden where birds make charming nests, kittens trick-or-treat in pumpkin patches, and so much more. In this whimsical coloring book for adults, you'll find colored examples to inspire you and new and enchanting fairytale art that you've never seen before. Bring imaginative scenes to life using your favorite coloring tools and express your creativity!

Kingdom
of
Curious
Creatures

SHIAWASE NO MENUET=*Menuet de bonheur* by Kanoko Egusa

Copyright © 2016 Kanoko Egusa

All rights reserved.

Original Japanese edition published by NATSUME SHUPPAN KIKAKU CO., LTD.

This English edition is published by arrangement with NATSUME SHUPPAN KIKAKU CO., LTD.,

Tokyo, in care of Tuttle-Mori Agency, Inc., Tokyo.

Copyright © 2022 Kanoko Egusa and New Design Originals Corporation, *www.d-originals.com*,

an imprint of Fox Chapel Publishing, 800-457-9112, 903 Square Street, Mount Joy, PA 17552.

Kingdom of Curious Creatures is a revised translation of the original Japanese book SHIAWASE NO MENUET=*Menuet de bonheur*.
This version published by New Design Originals Corporation, an imprint of Fox Chapel Publishing Company, Inc., Mount Joy, PA.

All colored samples were prepared by the publisher, not from guidance supplied by the author herself.

ISBN 978-1-4972-0570-3

COPY PERMISSION: The written instructions, photographs, designs, patterns, and projects in this publication are intended for the personal use of the reader and may be reproduced for that purpose only. Any other use, especially commercial use, is forbidden under law without the written permission of the copyright holder.
NOTE: The use of products and trademark names is for informational purposes only,
with no intention of infringement upon those trademarks.

Fox Chapel focuses on providing real value to our customers through the printing and book production process. We strive to select quality paper that is also eco-friendly. This book is printed on archival-quality, acid-free paper that can be expected to last for at least 200 years. It meets the minimum requirements of the American National Standard for Information Sciences—Permanence of Paper for Printed Library Materials, ANSI/NISO Z39.48-1992. This book is printed on paper produced from trees harvested from well-managed forests where measures are taken to protect wildlife, plants, and water quality.

We are always looking for talented authors.
To submit an idea, please send a brief inquiry to acquisitions@foxchapelpublishing.com.

Printed in Malaysia
Fourth printing